RECALLING THE EVENTS OF SOME OF STAFFORDSHIRE'S
MOST WELL KNOWN MURDERS

David J A Bell

BRADWELL
BOOKS

Published by Bradwell Books

11 Orgreave Close Sheffield S13 9NP

Email: books@bradwellbooks.co.uk

British Library Cataloguing in Publication Data: a catalogue record for this book is available from the British Library.

1st Edition

ISBN: 9781909914315

Print: Gomer Press, Llandysul, Ceredigion SA44 4JL

Design by: Andrew Caffrey

Typesetting by: Mark Titterton

Photograph Credits: Photography by the Author unless otherwise stated

CONTENTS

INTRODUCTION

In this book of Staffordshire murders, the stories range from 1797 to 1978. In the account from 1797, a wealthy pottery owner did not want his daughter to marry a lowly young doctor, which might sound strange to modern ears. Medicine was not regarded as a profession then, and the father forbade her from seeing her young man, a ban which led to a tragic outcome.

Another story tells how, in the severe winter of 1947, the boys living in an approved school near Eccleshall planned to escape after murdering the headmaster and stealing his car. The plan went awry, and they actually shot another teacher and had to escape in deep snow on foot. The following year, a young man in Codsall was assassinated by terrorists, who were actually aiming to kill his brother.

Unsurprisingly, Staffordshire's notorious poisoner, Dr William Palmer, puts in an appearance, as do the canal boatmen who murdered their passenger, a woman trying to get from Liverpool to join her husband in London. As she hadn't enough money to afford to travel by coach, she decided to take a cheaper journey by Pickford's canal boat, only to die tragically en route.

The murder of a newspaper boy in 1978 led to an infamous miscarriage of justice, described here. Two years earlier, a young lady was kidnapped for ransom by a ruthless man who had already killed three times during post office robberies. When things went wrong, he had no scruples about murdering her too.

Add in the poacher who was hanged twice, the murder of a headmistress in Burton, a tragic love triangle in Rudyard, and the bizarre case of a man who wanted to commit suicide by committing a murder and being hanged for it, and the reader will find much of interest in the crimes that have occurred in the county of Staffordshire.

David J A Bell

DEATH ON THE CANAL

CHRISTINA BROWN WAS BORN IN 1802, AND AS A YOUNG WOMAN SHE MARRIED A MUCH OLDER MAN, THOMAS INGLEBY. THOMAS WAS A POPULAR STAGE MAGICIAN, KNOWN AS THE EMPEROR OF ALL THE CONJURERS. HE TRAVELLED THE COUNTRY, PERFORMING HIS SHOWS. ONE OF HIS TRICKS WAS TO BORROW A POCKET WATCH FROM A MEMBER OF THE AUDIENCE, AND AFTER PUTTING INTO A CLOTH BAG, HE WOULD HAMMER IT TO BITS, THEN PRODUCE IT AS GOOD AS NEW. A MORE MACABRE ACT WAS TO CUT THE HEAD OFF A LIVE CHICKEN, BEFORE MAGICALLY RESTORING IT TO LIFE. THIS TRICK INVOLVED HAVING A SECOND LIVE CHICKEN ABOUT HIS PERSON. CHRISTINE TRAVELLED WITH HER HUSBAND, AND BECAME PART OF THE SHOW. ADDING SINGING AND DANCING TO THE PERFORMANCE, SHE ALSO TOOK PART IN THE CONJURING ACT.

Thomas died in 1832, leaving Christine an attractive young widow of 30. Eight years later she met and married a man of her own age, Robert Collins. They moved to Liverpool, where Christine soon found work as a seamstress, but there was no work for Robert. The following year he went to London, where he found work as an ostler, and obtained lodgings in Edgware Road. He immediately wrote to his wife, sending her a guinea for her journey to join him.

Finding that a guinea was not enough to travel to London by stagecoach, Christina discovered that she could go by canal for only 16 shillings. She booked her journey with Pickford and Co., and embarked from Preston Brook, the northern end of the Trent and Mersey Canal, on the evening of Saturday 15th June. The crew of the boat consisted of James Owen (the captain), George Thomas, William Ellis and a boy named Billy Musson.

The route should have taken her on the Trent and Mersey Canal through Stoke-on-Trent and Rugeley to Fradley Junction, where she would transfer to the Coventry Canal to Oxford, and then on to London. However, poor Christina never got any further than Rugeley. As soon as the boat set out, the three adult members of the crew began drinking and fantasising about the lone woman on board. They took great delight in embarrassing Christina by telling her in vulgar and lecherous language what they'd like to get up to with her.

When the boat reached Stoke-on-Trent, Christina complained to William Brookes, a Pickford's porter, about the behaviour of the crew. She even asked if was possible to transfer to a stage coach for the rest of the journey, but was told that none were available. To reassure Christina, Brookes arranged for his wife to travel on the boat with her for the next three-and-a-half miles. The men kept their behaviour down to a reasonable level while Mrs Brookes was present, but once she had left they were even worse than before, offering Christina drink and telling her they were going to 'meddle' with her.

At Stone, Christina again complained about her treatment, but a Trent and Mersey check clerk gave her the not very helpful advice that she could complain when she reached her destination. The journey continued, and Christina even took the extreme precaution of walking alongside the boat for a distance, rather than stay on board with the inebriated men. By midnight, the boat had reached Hoo Mill Lock, where the lock-keeper's wife was woken by the sound of a woman screaming. She looked out to see a woman sitting on top of the cabin, shouting, 'I will not go down. Do not attempt me!' The crew were on the towpath trying to get the woman to come down. The lock-keeper's wife asked one of the men who the woman was, and one of them replied that she was a passenger, whose husband was down below. This was an out-and-out lie, of course.

This was the last time Christina Collins was seen alive. Her body, floating face down in the canal, was spotted at 5am the next day by a boatman, Tom Grant. With the help of a passer-by, he pulled the body from the canal. It was taken to the Talbot Inn in Rugeley. When the Pickford agent heard what had occurred, he contacted the police. The inebriated crew were arrested when their boat reached Fazeley. After a coroner's inquest held in the Talbot Inn, all four of the crew were charged with assault and murder, although the boy, Billy Musson, was released without charge before the trial. At the initial hearing, the assault charges were dropped at the order of the judge, who said that there was no evidence to support the charge. The charge for murder still stood.

Evidence was given at the trial by William Brookes and his wife, the lock-keeper from Hoo Mill Lock, and others who had witnessed the distressed Christina Collins on her terrifying journey. The captain of another Pickford's boat stated that his vessel had been going along the

Contemporary illustrated broadsheet about the murder of Christina Collins

canal in the other direction. At 9pm the two boats crossed, and Owen had shouted to him, saying that he had a woman passenger on board. In vulgar terms he described what he'd like to do to her, adding that he would 'burke' her if he didn't get his way. He understood 'burke' meant to kill.

The grave of Christina Collins in Rugeley

All three men were found guilty and sentenced to be hanged. However, one of them, William Ellis, had his sentence commuted to transportation for 14 years and he was sent to a penal colony in Australia. The other men, James Owen and George Thomas, were hanged outside Stafford Road prison, in front of a crowd of ten thousand spectators. A public hanging was an entertainment, an exciting occasion with much drinking and merry-making. Men would take their families to watch, and would try to get a good vantage point for the gruesome spectacle.

The hangman was William Calcraft, who travelled the country conducting executions at £10 a time. His assistant, Tom Cheshire, got so drunk in the inns of Stafford on the night before the hanging that he failed to turn up. An assistant hangman was essential to the event, because the drop at that time was a short one, not sufficient to break the neck of the condemned man. One of the essential tasks of the assistant was to go below the staging and hasten death by pulling on the hanged man's feet. Calcraft appealed to the governor of Stafford prison, and a prisoner was found who was willing to assist him in return for having his own sentence quashed. The volunteer was called George Smith, and he took so well to his new career that he became a hangman in his own right, later officiating at the hanging of the notorious Dr Palmer of Rugeley, of whom more later.

YOU WILL NOT MARRY A DOCTOR

TO THE MODERN MIND, HAVING A GOOD-LOOKING YOUNG DOCTOR WISHING TO MARRY YOUR DAUGHTER WOULD NOT BE A SOCIAL PROBLEM. BUT IN 1797, ATTITUDES WERE DIFFERENT. TO A WELL-TO-DO FATHER, A DOCTOR WAS NOT A CATCH. DOCTORS WERE JUST TRADESMEN, AND OF LOW SOCIAL STANDING AT THAT.

John Wood was a wealthy pottery owner living in a large house between Burslem and Tunstall, close to his factory. When he called in the local doctor to attend to his ailing wife, it wasn't the elderly Dr Hickman who called, but his young assistant, Dr Thomas Milward Oliver. Young Dr Oliver saw to Mrs Wood competently enough, but it was Maria Wood, the pretty young daughter of the house, who caught his eye. Tom Oliver soon fell in love with the girl and it was obvious that Maria felt the same way about him.

The factory owner put up with the situation for a while, but when it became obvious that it wasn't a temporary infatuation but a deep and lasting affection, he was not happy. His daughter was certainly not going to marry someone with the lowly station and meagre income of a mere doctor. Dr Oliver was not a suitable suitor for his daughter. Tom was banned from the house, and Maria was forbidden from seeing him.

Although Tom and Maria did not see each other for over a year, their feelings for each other stayed as intense as ever. After a chance meeting in the summer of 1796, the couple began to meet secretly at an old watermill on John Wood's estate. When her father discovered that Maria was disobeying his instructions he was outraged. He surprised them at their trysting place, and lost his temper. The young doctor and the pottery owner exchanged angry words, and it developed into an exchange of blows.

After this, John Wood kept a much stricter eye on his daughter's whereabouts, and the young lovers were unable to meet. Tom began spending his evenings at the Turk's Head, in Burslem's Bucknall Road, drinking and brooding about the unfairness of the situation. He recalled that the pottery owner had sneered at his lowly status and poor income. When the other drinkers began to tease him about his feelings for Maria, even hinting that it was her money he was after, he began inwardly to seethe with bitterness and resentment.

Then his luck changed. John Wood's wife became unwell again and it was young Dr Oliver that she sent for. It seems possible that she didn't share her husband's dislike of the young man. She had certainly been happy with his medical skills and the way he had treated her during her earlier illness. The consequence of her decision was that Tom could now see Maria whenever he called to attend to her mother, although they could never be alone. They could see each other only when other people were present.

One of Tom Oliver's acquaintances at the Turk's Head was Ralph Johnson, who was a keen pistol shooter. Ralph taught Tom to shoot, and on the evening of Thursday 26th January, the young doctor borrowed two pistols from Ralph and took them home. The next day Dr Oliver presented himself at the Wood family house. He demanded to see the master of the house, but was told that Mr Wood was not available and that he was to present his bill to the chief clerk. Tom went to the clerk's office but continued to state that his business was personal, and he must see Mr Wood.

Eventually, Tom was allowed to wait in Wood's study until he was available. When an exasperated John Wood strode in to confront the young doctor, Tom Oliver raised a pistol and shot Wood in the chest. William Bathwell, Wood's foreman, who was also present, disarmed the doctor, preventing him from using the second pistol. Tom then said that he would not leave the house alive, put a quantity of poison into his mouth, and tried to swallow it. However, he immediately vomited it out again. When John Wood died of his wound three days later, Dr Tom Oliver was arrested and charged with murder.

At his trial, Tom stated that he had taken the pistol with the intention of shooting himself in front of John Wood, to show him what a desperate state he was in because of Wood's barring him from seeing Maria. Despite this argument, and despite a later plea of insanity, the court found him guilty of murder and the judge sentenced him to death. Actually, the fact that the jury took over an hour to come to their verdict in a case where none of the facts were in dispute indicates that they may have had some sympathy for the young, lovelorn doctor.

On the following Monday at 10.30am, Dr Thomas Oliver was hanged outside the gates of Stafford Gaol, in front of a large crowd of spectators. Afterwards, as the law required, his body was cut open and put on public display.

KIDNAP AND MURDER

DONALD NAPPEY MARRIED AT EIGHTEEN, AND AT NINETEEN HE WAS CALLED UP FOR NATIONAL SERVICE. HE BECAME AN INFANTRY MARKSMAN AND SERVED IN CYPRUS, ADEN AND KENYA, BEFORE RETURNING TO CIVILIAN LIFE. HE BOUGHT A TAXI FROM A MAN NAMED NEILSON. NAPPEY THEN CHANGED HIS OWN SURNAME TO NEILSON AFTER YEARS OF RESENTMENT OVER THE BANTER HE'D RECEIVED FROM HIS ARMY COMRADES. HE WAS STILL OBSESSED WITH MILITARY MATTERS AND FORCED HIS FAMILY TO TAKE PART IN WAR GAMES ON DISUSED ARMY BASES. REPLICA GUNS WERE NOT ENOUGH FOR NEILSON, SO IN 1971 HE BROKE INTO A HOUSE AND STOLE THREE SHOTGUNS.

In February 1974, he began a campaign of armed robbery, specialising in raiding sub-post offices. He was quite prepared to use violence. He shot dead three sub-postmasters – Donald Skepper, Derek Astin and Sidney Grayland – in an eight-month period. He also pistol-whipped and tied up Mr Grayland's wife Peggy. She was able to give the police a description of a dark-haired man in his late thirties. Because he always dressed in black, and was quite prepared to kill without compunction, the press decided to dub him the Black Panther. This was shameful: an insult to a graceful and beautiful animal. It also lent unwarranted glamour to a man who killed as part of his unglamorous chosen career.

Donald Neilson

Robbery was not proving to be as financially rewarding as Neilson had hoped, and he recalled that in May 1972 the national press reported the case of a contested will. Donald Neilson was not interested in the rights and wrongs of the case, but he did mentally file the information that a young teenage girl had inherited a large sum – £80,000 – from her father. Neilson decided to kidnap the girl for ransom. Early in 1975 he decided to put his plan into action. He knew of a place in North Staffordshire where he could hide Lesley Whittle: a drainage shaft beneath a park in Kidsgrove.

When Dorothy Whittle went into her daughter's room on the morning of Tuesday 15th January, Lesley was missing. Her mother's disquiet increased when she realised that the only clothes missing were a nightdress, a dressing gown and slippers. It meant that 17-year-old Lesley had disappeared without any outdoor or daytime clothing.

Dorothy's son Ronald came to the house and he found a message from the kidnapper in an empty chocolate box which had been placed on top of a vase. The message was neither hand-written nor typed; it was stamped onto Dymo tape. The chilling words read: NO POLICE £50000 RANSOM BE READY TO DELIVER FIRST EVENING WAIT FOR TELEPHONE CALL AT SWAN SHOPPING CENTRE TELEPHONE BOX 6PM TO 1AM IF NO CALL RETURN FOLLOWING EVENING YOU MUST FOLLOW INSTRUCTIONS WITHOUT ARGUMENT FROM THE TIME YOU ANSWER THE TELEPHONE YOU ARE ON A TIME LIMIT IF POLICE OR TRICKS DEATH. A second Dymo tape told them how the £50,000 was to be made up of used £5 and £1 notes.

Despite the opening words of the first message, the West Mercia police were called in. The officer in charge was Chief Superintendent Bob Booth, a detective who had successfully solved every one of the seventy murder cases he had investigated. Bob Booth knew that the man who had kidnapped the girl was a callous criminal, but even he could not have guessed just how vicious the man could be. Lesley had already been taken to the drainage shaft under Bathpool Park in Kidsgrove, where she was standing on a narrow ledge and tethered by a wire noose around her neck.

The plan was to keep the police involvement a secret. Bob Booth arranged for the £50,000 ransom money to be withdrawn from the bank, and for Ronald Whittle to take it to the Swan Shopping Centre as the kidnapper had instructed. However, things went badly wrong. News of the kidnapping was broadcast on the television news at 9pm, and a police officer aborted the procedure. Bob Booth was horrified and furious. The operation had been aborted without reference to him, and he knew that the television news broadcast might mean the death of the kidnapped girl.

Bob Booth decided to send Ronald to the same phone box on the following evening, hoping that the kidnapper would ring again, but the officer was disgusted to find the kiosk surrounded by reporters and photographers.

On the same evening as the second unsuccessful visit to the phone box, an apparently unconnected crime took place 30 miles away in Dudley. A British Rail security guard approached a man who was lurking near the freightliner depot. The man shot him down, then tried to shoot him again at point-blank range. Fortunately the gun failed to fire this time and the man ran off.

Examination of the bullet proved it to be the same type as those used to kill the sub-postmasters.

In the meantime, the kidnapper had been in contact again. The transport manager at the Whittle coach company answered a call, which he knew from the pips was from a call box. To his joy he heard the voice of Lesley Whittle. As he tried to speak to her, her voice continued and he realised he was listening to a tape recording, which said, 'Mum, you are to go to Kidsgrove Post Office phone box. The instructions are going to be inside. I'm okay but there are to be no police and no tricks, okay.'

The police wired up Ronald Whittle with a microphone and he set off for North Staffordshire. At Kidsgrove he found the post office and began to search the phone box. Eventually he located a message, which told him to go to a particular point in Bathpool Park at midnight and look for a flashing light. He would find a torch with further instructions fastened onto it. Ronald immediately drove to the park but to his despair he was unable to find any flashing light. Once again the trail had turned cold. Bob Booth sanctioned Scotland Yard officers to make a discreet search of Bathpool Park but they reported that they had found nothing.

A week after the Dudley shooting, the police found an abandoned stolen car with false number plates, only a few hundred yards away from where the incident had occurred. Evidence in the car – including more Dymo tapes and a second cassette tape with Lesley Whittle's voice – proved that it was not only connected with the post office shootings but also with the Lesley Whittle kidnapping. For the first time, the police knew that the kidnapper was a man who had already killed three times.

On 7th March, children playing in Bathpool Park found pieces of Dymo tape and a torch by the entrance to a drainage shaft that they knew as 'the Glory Hole'. There were actually three of these drainage shafts and Bob Booth ordered them to be searched. At the third, on a metal grille 50 feet down, they saw a mattress, a blanket and a sleeping bag. DC Philip Maskery went down to the narrow shelf, and by the light of his torch he caught sight of a blue dressing gown. He shone his torch further down the shaft and saw the body of Lesley Whittle, hanging from a metal cord round her neck.

As the death had occurred in Kidsgrove, Staffordshire Police now took over the case. Bob Booth fought to continue with his team but he was sidelined and no longer in charge of the case. His disquiet was increased when he learned that a witness had come forward with evidence that a Staffordshire Police panda car was in Bathpool Park at the time when Ronald Whittle was trying to make contact with the kidnapper. Peter Shorto, a local DJ, and his girlfriend had been parked in the park at 2.45am but their courting was interrupted. First a torch was flashed on and off a few yards in front of their car, which Peter thought might have been someone walking a dog. Then headlights swept across the park, and a car pulled up nearby. The driver lit a cigarette, and Peter commented to his girlfriend that it was just a policeman stopping for a smoke. Fifteen minutes later, a van drove into the park, parked in front of Peter's car, flashed its headlights, then left, driving off at speed.

Bob Booth concluded that the presence of a police car in Bathpool Park that night had panicked the kidnapper, and that this had caused him to return to the drainage shaft that night to push the tethered girl off the ledge. Although Staffordshire Police denied that any of their cars were in the park that night, Chief Superintendent Booth remained sceptical.

It was mid-December before Donald Neilson was captured, and his arrest occurred only because he had gone back to robbing post offices. Two Nottinghamshire police officers were parked when one of them, PC Tony White, spotted a man acting suspiciously near a post office. His colleague, PC Stuart Mackenzie, drove up to the man and Tony White began to question him. The man began by saying his name was John Moxon, but suddenly produced a shotgun. He ordered PC White to get into the back of the car, then climbed in next to the driver, pointing the gun at his chest.

After driving for some time, PC Mackenzie decided that he had to take some action. As they neared the village of Rainworth, he suddenly swerved right then left, braking at the same time. The gun went off, and Stuart threw himself from the car. He heard Tony shouting that he had been shot in the hand, and hurried round the car to help. He saw that Tony was holding the gunman round the neck and was thumping him with his elbow. As the two officers struggled with Moxon, they were joined by a local man, Roy Morris, who had raced from a nearby chip shop to help them. They managed to handcuff the gunman and chained him to some railings. More locals came out to help, and in the end the two police officers had to protect their captive from being beaten up by the civilians.

In Moxon's holdall the police found torches, knives, razor blades, a bottle of ammonia and a black hood. After two days, Moxon admitted that his name was really Donald Neilson. In the attic of his Bradford home, the police discovered maps and car keys, more black hoods, a sawn-off shotgun, and the Dymo machine that had punched out the messages. The police were sickened and disgusted when they also found a model of a black panther. Donald Neilson had obviously revelled in the press attention and the nickname the press had given him.

At his trial in July 1976, Neilson was charged with thirteen violent crimes, four of them murders. He admitted that he had robbed the post offices where the men had been shot. He also admitted that he had kidnapped Lesley Whittle and held her in the drainage shaft in Kidsgrove. Neilson seemed to enjoy his time in court, and willingly donned his black balaclava mask, showed how he had held his shotgun, and even demonstrated how he had put the wire round Lesley's neck. He claimed that he had not killed Lesley deliberately, but had accidentally pushed her off the ledge. Whether any of the jury might have believed this version of the events is doubtful, but he then stretched credulity even further by claiming that his gun went off accidentally in each of the robberies where a man died.

He was not believed and the jury took only 90 minutes to find him guilty of the kidnap and murder of Lesley Whittle, and of the murders of the three sub-postmasters. He received five life sentences, and was told by the Home Secretary that he would never be released. He died in prison in 2011.

HEADLESS IN HEDNESFORD

ON WEDNESDAY 19TH FEBRUARY 1919, ELIZABETH GASKIN RECEIVED A NOTE FROM HER ESTRANGED HUSBAND, TOM. IT WAS DELIVERED BY A WORKMATE OF TOM'S FROM WEST CANNOCK COLLIERY, WHO HAD BEEN DRINKING WITH HIM IN A HEDNESFORD PUB. THE MESSAGE READ: 'MEET ME ROUND THE POOL AT ONCE – IMPORTANT.' THE 23-YEAR-OLD WOMAN LEFT HER SIX-MONTH OLD BABY WITH HER MOTHER, AND SET OFF TO WALK TO THE POOL NEAR THE CANNOCK COLLIERY OFFICES.

The couple were seen talking by two colliery officials. They seemed to be arguing. Elizabeth and Tom walked towards the wood, then split up, Tom going into the wood and Elizabeth returning towards the home she shared with her mother in Brindley Heath.

When Elizabeth failed to come home, her mother notified the police, who searched the wood. Tom Gaskin was questioned the next day, and he claimed he hadn't seen Elizabeth at all. On Friday afternoon, he was arrested and taken in for questioning. On Sunday, he told an inspector where they would find his wife's body. He travelled in a taxi with police officers to the gasworks in Victoria Street where he led the officers over a five-foot wall. He pointed to the water-filled tank surrounding the base of the gasholder, and told them, 'She is in there.' He warned them that they would need two drags, because Elizabeth was in pieces.

He was correct. They first fished out her headless body, and two days later they recovered the head. Gaskin told the police that he had met up with his wife a few minutes after they had been seen parting on the Wednesday afternoon. Elizabeth had suggested that they should go back to her mother's house to discuss their marital problems. When he refused, Elizabeth had started to cry, and he had seized her by the throat and strangled her.

He initially left her body in the wood, but returned later that night to dismember it. He had managed to cut off the head, but failed when he tried to cut off her limbs. He hid the torso in a culvert, and threw the head and clothing into the tank under the gasometer. On the Thursday night, after being questioned by the police, he had recovered the body from the culvert, weighed it down and taken it to the place where he had disposed of the head.

Thomas Gaskin's trial was held in Stafford in July 1919. The prosecutor began by telling the jury, 'I shudder to

Gruesome contemporary postcard
issued after the murder of Elizabeth Gaskin

think I have to present to you a case which is so full of ferocious detail.' He described the injuries to Elizabeth's body as a 'gruesome catalogue of the most savage cruelty'. Elizabeth's mother, Emily Talbot, gave evidence that Tom and Elizabeth had married in 1913, but that they were living apart by 1916 when Thomas had joined the Royal Engineers. Elizabeth had two children, and had confessed to her mother that one of them was not her husband's. Despite this, Tom and Elizabeth had been on good terms when he came home on leave, and he had agreed to bring up both children as his own.

The defence counsel argued that the nature of the crime and the brutal way in which the body had been mangled proved that Gaskin could not have been sane at the time. Tom's mother said that he had always been strange in his manners, and had tried to strangle himself with a scarf as a child. His strangeness had been much worse when he came home after the war.

Two former army comrades, Charles Dawson and Ernest Woodhall, gave evidence of the recklessness shown by Tom Gaskin on the front line, including going backwards and forwards among flying shells and falling buildings. They also informed the court that he had been blown up by a German mine, and had not behaved normally since.

Despite this evidence about Tom Gaskin's terrible experiences during the war and his strange behaviour, the jury decided to reject the plea of insanity. They took less than 15 minutes to find him guilty of the murder of his wife. Thomas was sentenced to death, and was hanged in Winson Green prison in Birmingham a month later.

THE APPROVED SCHOOL BREAKOUT

IT WAS THE EARLY MONTHS OF 1947, AND THE 65 YOUNG MALE RESIDENTS OF STANDON FARM APPROVED SCHOOL, NEAR ECCLESHALL, WERE FED UP. ONE FACTOR WAS THE SEVERE WEATHER. THE WINTER OF 1946–47 WAS ONE OF THE COLDEST ON RECORD, AND FROZEN SNOW HAD COVERED THE COUNTRY FOR MONTHS. ANOTHER FACTOR WAS THAT THE HEADMASTER, MR THOMAS DAWSON, HAD DECIDED THAT 12 MONTHS AT THE REFORM SCHOOL WAS INSUFFICIENT TIME FOR ANY OF THE BOYS TO BENEFIT FROM THE TRAINING THERE, AND SO WOULD NOT ISSUE A LICENCE FOR ANY BOY TO RETURN HOME AFTER ONLY ONE YEAR.

The school had been built in 1885 as a home for waifs and strays, but in 1936 it had been turned into a residential school for boys between 13 and 16 who were in trouble with the law, or who were deemed to be out of control.

In February ten of the older boys devised a desperate plan of escape. They would murder the headmaster and steal his car, then drive away to freedom. One of the boys was a natural leader. He was an NCO in the school army cadet corps. He organised his followers into stealing the food

Standon Farm Approved School
(Staffordshire Police Museum)

and warm clothing they would need for the great escape. The original plan was to time the event to coincide with the monthly staff meeting, when there would be only one teacher on duty. However, they became too impatient to wait, and so it was on Saturday 15th February that they decided to put the plan into action.

One group of boys broke into the cadet corps armoury and stole three Lee Enfield rifles, while a second group forced the door into the headmaster's study where the ammunition was kept. At 1.30pm, four of the boys were in the school bathroom, loading bullets into the rifles, when they were interrupted. The door opened and there stood Peter Fieldhouse, the 21-year-old assistant gardening master. As he began to ask what they thought they were doing, one boy fired a rifle at him but missed. He then fired a second shot, which wounded the man and brought him down. As the young teacher lay helpless on the floor, the boy calmly reloaded the rifle and shot him at point-blank range in the chest.

The ten conspirators then abandoned their original plan to steal the headmaster's car, dropped their weapons and left the school on foot. They made their way through heavy snowdrifts across the fields to Stableford, where they got onto the railway line. This made for easier going, and they began to walk towards Madeley, but they were spotted by a signalman.

Back at Standon Farm School, Mr Dawson had sent for the police and a doctor, but it was too late. Peter Fieldhouse had been fatally wounded, and by 2pm he had died of his injuries. A massive police hunt for the boys was put into operation, cars searching the snow-covered lanes and police on foot searching the fields and the railway line. At 5.30pm, two police officers, PCs Sumnall and Holleran, caught the boys on the railway line between Madeley and Crewe. Nine of the boys were arrested without problem, but the tenth made a run for it across the fields with PC Luther Sumnall in pursuit. It must have been almost like a slow-motion chase, as they were both running through deep snowdrifts. After twenty minutes, the boy was caught, and all ten fugitives were taken to the police station in Newcastle-under-Lyme.

There they were questioned by Detective Superintendant Tom Lockley. When they were unwilling to say which of them had shot Peter Fieldhouse, Tom Lockley charged all ten with the murder. The boys conferred among

PC Luther Sumnall
(Staffordshire Police Museum)

themselves and elected a spokesman, who stated, 'I will speak for the lot and tell the truth. We got fed up with school and we planned to shoot the headmaster. We were going to pinch the headmaster's car and some stores and get away. We planned it for the next staff meeting but it was too long to wait.'

The trial of the ten boys was held a month later in Stafford. In the witness box, Thomas Dawson stated that eight of the ten boys were mentally subnormal. PC Luther Sumnall described how he had arrested nine of the boys on the railway line, and the tenth 20 minutes later after a chase. A statement made by the ringleader was read to the court. It stated,'Between 1.30 and 2pm, I was in the bathroom at Standon Hall School with three rifles when Mr Fieldhouse walked through the door and asked what we were doing. I pulled the trigger and shot him. That shot missed. I pulled the trigger and shot again and he fell to the ground. I reloaded and shot at him again. Then we all made a run for it.'

The jury reached their verdict after just 30 minutes. Four of the boys were found guilty of murdering Peter Fieldhouse and were sentenced to be detained during His Majesty's Pleasure. Five others were found guilty of conspiracy to murder and were sent to borstal. One boy was acquitted. Following an inquiry, the headmaster was dismissed and Standon Farm Approved School was closed down. Both the police officers who had caught the fugitives were awarded a commendation.

WHO KILLED CARL BRIDGEWATER?

AT FIVE O'CLOCK ON THE AFTERNOON OF TUESDAY 19TH SEPTEMBER 1978, DR ANGUS MACDONALD CALLED AT YEW TREE FARM TO SEE MARY POOLE, WHO HAD BEEN IN HOSPITAL RECENTLY. HE PARKED IN THE FARMYARD AND WALKED THROUGH THE OPEN WICKET GATE TO THE BACK DOOR. HE NOTICED THE EVENING PAPER IN THE BOX BY THE DOOR, BUT WAS ALARMED TO SEE THAT THE DOOR'S PAINTWORK WAS BATTERED AND THE WOOD AROUND THE LOCK HAD BEEN CHIPPED AWAY. IMMEDIATELY, THE DOCTOR GUESSED THAT THE FARMHOUSE HAD BEEN BROKEN INTO. HE WENT INTO THE HOUSE AND SAW THE HORRIFIC SIGHT OF A BOY'S DEAD BODY SLUMPED ON THE SETTEE, HIS NEWSPAPER BAG STILL SLUNG OVER HIS BACK.

The dead boy was thirteen-year-old Carl Bridgewater, who delivered the Express and Star every evening on his bike. His paper round was mainly in the village of Wordsley, though he always finished with a ride down Lawnswood Road to deliver papers to three outlying houses, including Yew Tree Farm. He had been seen on his round at about 4pm.

At 7.30pm, Mary Poole and her cousin Fred Jones returned from a day trip into Shropshire. When they arrived home they were amazed to find the farm drive full of police cars. After the police had informed Mary and Fred about what had occurred, Dr Macdonald took the shaken pair to his own home to spend the night. The

Yew Tree Farm where Carl Bridgewater was murdered
(picture: Express & Star)

cousins lived together at Yew Tree Farm, though the land was farmed by a neighbouring farmer, Hubert Wilkes.

At 10pm, the boy's body was removed to the mortuary at Wordsley Hospital, where it was identified by his father. Carl had been shot through the left side of the head by a single bullet from a shotgun from a distance of less than four feet.

Fred Jones confirmed that the house at Yew Tree Farm was full of antiques, some of them quite valuable. He mentioned to the police that £70 had disappeared in April from an envelope at the bottom of a drawer in his bedroom. He also recalled that a few weeks previously, he and Mary had been to Birmingham, leaving the door key under a slate on the coalhouse window ledge. On his return, Fred found the key lying in a different position.

The police were interested to learn that Fred's dog, Skip, had been left in the kitchen when the cousins left home on the morning of the killing but was found by the police officers shut in the scullery. This raised the question of whether the intruder might have been someone the dog knew. Was the reason the paperboy had been killed because he recognised the robber? Chief Supt Bob Stewart was quoted in the Express & Star as saying, 'I tend to go for the view that the motive was that he could have recognised his assailant.' It appeared at this stage that the police were definitely seeking a local man.

But it might have been more than one man. Every room in the house had been ransacked. Outside in the yard and orchard, the police found a number of abandoned items that had been taken from the house, and Carl Bridgewater's bike was found dumped in the pigsty. Among the items still missing were two brass candlesticks, an oak tantalus and three cut-glass decanters, a ladies' pocket watch, a heavy silver watch chain, and two pairs of gold and silver cufflinks.

A witness named Roger Edwards told the police that at 2.50pm, he had seen a pale blue Vauxhall Viva turn into the farm drive. He said that the driver was a man of about 55 with wavy hair. The man was wearing a dark blue uniform and looked like a police officer or a fireman. The police began to seek information about any uniformed men who drove a blue Vauxhall Viva. Eventually they came up with the name of Bert Spencer, an ambulance driver based in Stourbridge. His name had been given to them earlier in the investigation as a man who bought and sold antiques. At his interview, Spencer said that he was a collector of antiques, but had never been a dealer. However, this was proved incorrect: Spencer had at one time been a partner in an antique shop.

He also had several connections with Carl Bridgewater and Yew Tree Farm. Between 1970 and 1975, Bert Spencer had been a close neighbour of the Bridgewater family, and Carl would have known him. He knew the farmhouse and its owners well, and he had been inside the farmhouse on several occasions. He knew, and was known by, Skip the dog.

However, police interest in Bert Spencer ended suddenly when on Friday 30th November an isolated farmhouse in Worcestershire was robbed. Two masked men, one armed with a sawn-off shotgun, broke into Chapel Farm, Romsley, and demanded money from the elderly family who lived there. They stole £200, and made their getaway in a green Austin 1100 driven by a third man. A window cleaner noted the car's registration number.

The similarities between this raid and the robbery/ murder at Yew Tree Farm struck the police immediately: an isolated farmhouse, elderly occupants, three robbers armed with a shotgun. Surely, these were no mere coincidences. When the car registration was traced to Linda Galvin of Northfields, Birmingham, the police were even more convinced. The police visited Linda and found that 25-year-old Vincent Hickey had been living with her since August. Vincent was serving a suspended sentence for deception linked to a robbery in Hertfordshire, and he was a member of a close-knit family with links to the Birmingham underworld. All other lines of investigation were dropped as the police began a hunt for Vincent Hickey.

When Vincent heard that the police were linking the Chapel Farm robbery with the Carl Bridgewater killing, he went into Bromsgrove police station and gave himself up. He was never a free man again.

Vincent was questioned by officers of various police forces, including detectives from Staffordshire. He stated that his cousin Michael had taken part in the robbery at Chapel Farm with two other men. His own involvement had been restricted to lending them a car. Vincent refused to give any other names at first, but two days later he mentioned the names of Jimmy Robinson and Pat Molloy. The police were quite excited by this information. Robinson was known to them and had served a suspended sentence for involvement in a robbery at a meat store in Tamworth, and Molloy was a frequent drinking companion of his. When Robinson went into Harborne Lane police station on 6th December to report for bail, he was arrested and charged with the Chapel Farm robbery. In the early hours of the next day, Jimmy Robinson admitted his part in the raid, and took the police to where his shotgun and eleven cartridges were hidden. He still denied any connection with the Yew Tree Farm killing. Pat Molloy, a 50-year-old carpenter, was arrested on 8th December and charged with involvement in the Tamworth robbery. The police continued to seek Michael Hickey.

The three men in custody – Vincent Hickey, Jimmy Robinson and Pat Molloy – were questioned at length over the next few days. Between 7th and 10th December, 38 separate interviews took place. Unfortunately, these occurred before the routine tape-recording of interviews became a legal requirement, and the police notes were made after, rather than during, the interviews. There were no solicitors present, and the three suspects were held in solitary confinement when not being questioned.

Pat Molloy was anxious to please and to co-operate with the police. After three days of questioning, in which he denied taking any part in the Yew Tree Farm robbery, he finally said that he had been there with the Hickey cousins and Jimmy Robinson. However, when Molloy was actually taken by the police to Yew Tree Farm, he failed to recognise the location. There were also several anomalies in his statement – he was extremely vague about the details and he made no mention of the dog at the farm – so the police were hopeful that Vincent Hickey and Jimmy Robinson would break down and confess once they saw Molloy's statement. However, both men dismissed it as a pack of lies, and the police realised that they would need to rely on Molloy's very confused and often contradictory statement to make their case at a trial.

Michael Hickey, aged sixteen, was arrested in December. He immediately confessed to taking part in the Chapel

Farm raid and another robbery, but denied that he had anything to do with the events at Yew Tree Farm. All four men were charged with murder and appeared at Stafford Crown Court the following October. Witnesses who were called said that they had seen a blue estate car near the farm on the day of the murder. This was important to the prosecution case, as Vincent Hickey had once owned a car of this type, but the jury did not hear from other witnesses, including Roger Edwards, who had seen the Vauxhall Viva being driven by a man in uniform at 2.50pm.

Although the law held that Pat Molloy's statement was not evidence against anyone except himself – and the judge was meticulous in explaining this legal point to the jury – its influence was considerable. The jury retired at 3pm on 8th November, and returned the next day to bring in verdicts of guilty of murder against Jimmy Robinson, Vincent Hickey and Michael Hickey. Pat Molloy was found guilty of manslaughter. Robinson and Vincent Hickey were sentenced to life imprisonment, with a recommendation that each serve 25 years. Michael Hickey was to be detained at Her Majesty's Pleasure, and Pat Molloy got twelve years.

However, the case of the Bridgewater Four, as the convicted men came to be known – they became the Bridgewater Three when Pat Molloy died in 1981 – has been a controversial one ever since. None of the three has ever admitted their guilt, though their life in prison would have been more comfortable if they had. Michael Hickey spent 89 days on the roof of Gartree Prison, in Leicestershire, protesting his innocence. The fact that his fellow prisoners supported and fed him throughout this period does not of course prove his innocence, though it does indicate that the other prisoners believed him. The treatment of convicted child-killers by other prisoners is not normally very sympathetic.

For the next 19 years, all calls for a reopening of the case of the convicted men were turned down. Television programmes were made, books written, MPs on both sides of the House took up the cause, and some members of the original jury, including the foreman, came out publicly to renounce their original verdict and to support the case for a new inquiry. In 1996, Michael Chance, the official who had handled the prosecution for the Director of Public Prosecutions, stated that he thought it 'a disturbing error' that certain evidence – particularly the fact that the fingerprints found on Carl Bridgewater's bike did not match the prints of any of the accused – was not made available to the defence at the time of the trial. Mr Chance said that this caused him a great deal of concern and militated towards the Home Secretary giving further consideration to a new referral to the Court of Appeal. Following these comments, Home Secretary Michael Howard announced that the case would be allowed to go back to the Court of Appeal.

This appeal was successful. The judges stated that the police officers' account of Pat Molloy's confession 'was most improbable, if not impossible'. New evidence put before the court indicated that Hickey's signature appeared to be consistent with that of DC John Perkins, and that its wording was that of DC Graham Leeke. Lord Justice Roche stated that one of the officers, DC Perkins, 'was prepared to resort to deceit to obtain evidence'. They also found that the evidence against Michael Hickey was 'of such a tenuous character that a reasonable jury properly directed could not convict on it', and that in the case of Jimmy Robinson there were concerns about identification against him and the treatment of his alibi. The three surviving members of the Bridgewater Four were released, after spending eighteen years in prison.

A bizarre postscript to the case took place a month after the end of the trial when the ambulance driver interviewed by police earlier in the Bridgewater case shot dead a local farmer in a farmhouse just a few hundred yards from Yew Tree Farm. Hubert Wilkes and his daughter had invited the ambulance driver and his wife over to visit them. Suddenly Bert Spencer left the room, returned with a shotgun, and shot Hubert Wilkes dead. At his trial in June 1980, Bert Spencer claimed that he had blacked out and could not recall the events at Holloway Farm. He was found guilty of murdering Hubert Wilkes and sentenced to life imprisonment.

ASSASSINATION IN CODSALL

MAJOR ROY FARRAN HAD GIVEN HEROIC SERVICE DURING THE WAR, AS A MEMBER OF THE SAS, SERVING IN ITALY, TUNISIA, GREECE AND FRANCE. HE WAS AWARDED THE DISTINGUISHED SERVICE ORDER, THE MILITARY CROSS AND TWO BARS, THE FRENCH CROIX DE GUERRE AND THE AMERICAN LEGION OF MERIT. AFTER THE WAR, HE STOOD AS A CANDIDATE FOR THE DUDLEY AND STOURBRIDGE CONSTITUENCY IN THE 1945 GENERAL ELECTION, THOUGH HE WAS NOT ELECTED. HE ALSO WROTE A BOOK, WINGED DAGGER: ADVENTURES ON SPECIAL SERVICE. THIS WAS ACCEPTED BY COLLINS AND WAS DUE TO BE PUBLISHED IN 1948.

He then became an undercover agent in Palestine, organising and leading the Q Squads, formed to investigate and sabotage the activities of the Lehi, otherwise known as the Stern Gang. This was a Jewish organisation formed by Avraham Stern in 1940, which had split off from the Irgun militant group. The Stern Gang were fanatically anti-British during the war, and had even invited help from the German Nazis to drive the British out of Palestine. They regarded themselves as freedom fighters for an Israeli state, but to the British they were violent terrorists. Although Stern himself was killed in 1942, his movement continued, assassinating Lord Moyne, a British minister of state, in 1944. After the war, they continued to use bombs and bullets to achieve their aims.

Roy Farran's Q Squads were formed to combat the terrorists at their own game and using their own tactics. On 6th May 1947, a fifteen-year-old boy, Alexander Rubowitz, was spotted distributing pro-Stern literature. He was last seen being bundled into a car and driven away by members of the Q Squads. The boy's parents were informed that he was 'presumed dead'. One of the men who had kidnapped the boy lost his hat during the struggle, and it was found at the scene. That hat had the letters F A – R A N (the fourth letter was missing) written inside it, and an eyewitness identified the man who had caught and abducted the boy as being Major Roy Farran.

In October, Major Farran was tried by a general court martial, charged with murdering the missing Alexander Rubowitz. A legal debate took place when Roy Farran's defence counsel objected to the use by the prosecution of material written by the accused man while in custody. The argument was that they were notes written as part of his defence preparation, so they ought to be privileged and therefore inadmissible as evidence. The court martial agreed and ruled that the notes could not be used against him. Buoyed by this ruling, the defence now argued that as the boy's body had never been found, there was no case against Farran. The court martial agreed and Roy Farran was acquitted. He returned to his home in Codsall, Staffordshire.

The Stern Gang never accepted the court martial's verdict and vowed that they would avenge the death of Alexander Rubowitz. It was on the morning of Monday 3rd May 1948, that a parcel was delivered to The Myron, Histons Hill, Codsall, the home of Roy Farran. Roy was away in Scotland with his police bodyguard at the time, so the parcel was received by his younger brother Rex, a twenty-six-year-old engineering draughtsman. Rex could tell from the shape and feel of the parcel that it contained a book. Assuming it was an advance copy of Roy's Winged Dagger, he began to open it. It wasn't Winged Dagger, however, but a copy of the Complete Works of Shakespeare.

Rex Farran – back row far right

The house in Histons Hill after the explosion
(picture: Express & Star)

As Rex opened the book, a bomb inside it blew up, causing tremendous injuries to his abdomen and legs. He was rushed to Wolverhampton Royal Hospital, but he died two hours later. The booby-trapped parcel had been posted in the East End of London. The day after the murder, a British news agency in Paris received a phone call from a man claiming to be speaking on behalf of the Stern Gang. He said that the killing had been in revenge for the murder of Alexander Rubowitz.

If the message was genuine, and there seems no reason to doubt it, then the organisation had murdered not the man they held responsible, but his younger brother, a cheerful and likeable young man with absolutely no connection with the politics of the Middle East. Rex, a keen footballer in the works team, was described as a man without an enemy in the world. Joan Cooper, whose husband worked with Rex Farran at the Boulton & Paul aircraft factory, said that Rex was a wonderful young man, always smiling. She added: 'What sort of people could do that to someone like Rex?'

Rex Farran's funeral was held in Codsall on Friday 7th May, and was attended by his parents and brothers, his colleagues from Boulton & Paul, his football teammates and his many friends. Major Roy Farran later emigrated to Canada, where he became a newspaper proprietor in Calgary.

Roy Farran kneels at his brother's grave
(picture: Express & Star)

THE SOLDIER AND THE HEADMISTRESS

IN JULY 1951, ARMY DESERTER JOHN FENTON WENT AWOL FROM THE PIONEER CORPS IN LOCKERBIE, SCOTLAND. HE WAS TWENTY YEARS OLD, BUT LOOKED MUCH YOUNGER. BORN AND RAISED IN DERBY, HE MADE HIS WAY DOWN TO THE MIDLANDS, THOUGH IT WAS ENTIRELY BY CHANCE THAT HE FOUND HIMSELF IN BURTON-UPON-TRENT. THERE, HE BROKE INTO A DETACHED HOUSE IN THE GROUNDS OF BURTON GIRLS' HIGH SCHOOL, THINKING THAT IT WAS EMPTY. HE INTENDED TO CAMP OUT THERE FOR A FEW DAYS, STEALING FOOD AND GENERALLY MAKING HIMSELF AT HOME.

The house, known as The Woodlands, was in fact the residence of Miss Winifred Mulley, the 52-year-old headmistress of the school. The school had broken up on 25th July, and Miss Mulley had been due to go away on holiday on Monday 30th, but she had decided to postpone her trip until after the bank holiday.

On Tuesday 1st August, the cleaner, Emily Plummer, arrived at The Woodlands at 9.45am. She was surprised that there was a dirty cup and saucer on the kitchen table. That was most unlike Miss Mulley. Nevertheless, Mrs Plummer washed them up and continued with her duties. The door to the headmistress's bedroom was locked, and when she knocked there was no reply. Eventually she decided to try a key from another bedroom, and it fitted. She unlocked the door and went in. Miss Mulley was in bed with an eiderdown pulled right over her. There was also blood on the floor.

Realising that something was seriously wrong, the cleaner went for help. The head gardener, George Chatterton, returned with her, and he pulled back the eiderdown. Miss Mulley was dead, with a small penknife protruding from her neck. When the police arrived, it was found that Miss Mulley had severe head wounds, as well as the small stab wound caused by the penknife. On the bedside table were two unopened tins: one of sausages, the other of anchovies. The pearl-handled penknife used to stab Miss Mulley was her own, and was usually kept on the bedside table.

Emily Plummer told the police that she had seen Miss Mulley and chatted with her for twenty minutes on the previous day. George Chatterton recalled that he had found a young man sleeping rough in one of the greenhouses on Monday morning. The man had said that he had missed the last bus to Derby, and then left the premises. The police managed to establish that the same young man had been seen in the nearby villages of Repton and Newton Solney, on the Monday. They issued a description of him which said that he looked about sixteen or seventeen, of medium build with slim hips, light brown hair, and wearing a blue pinstriped suit and scruffy brown shoes. Despite the good suit, he was said to be of 'rather unkempt appearance'.

A man answering the description had been seen by a porter at Burton Railway station in the early hours of Tuesday morning, some twelve hours before Miss Mulley's body had been found. He had used two pound notes to buy a single ticket to Bristol, and caught the

The Woodlands, where Miss Mulley was murdered
(Burton Mail)

12.40am train. A week later the police announced that were looking for a twenty-year-old army deserter named John Fenton, in connection with the murder of Winifred Mulley. Fenton was arrested by Sussex Police, who found him sleeping under a boat on the beach at Worthing. He was brought back to Burton and charged with murder.

He made a statement saying that he had deserted from the army because he was afraid of retaliation from a fellow soldier whom he had reported for stealing his clothes. He had gone to the pictures in Carlisle and slept in a field. The next day he had walked to Penrith and slept in a wood. He had used all his money, 10 shillings, on a bus fare to Kendal, where he had slept in a lorry. When the driver returned, he had stayed hidden in the lorry, which had brought him to Burton. He had slept in a greenhouse, then walked to Repton and back. He returned to the school grounds, intending to sleep in the greenhouse again, but saw what he thought was an empty house. He entered by the kitchen window and began to search for food. He ate some bread and jam, then stole two tins and a tin opener from the pantry. He went upstairs and had almost reached the bathroom when a woman in pyjamas came out of a bedroom. She had seized him and demanded to know what he doing.

He panicked and began hitting the woman on the face and head with one of the tins he had taken from the pantry. When she passed out, he laid her down on the bed. He then picked up a penknife from the bedside table and stuck it in her neck. He then left, after locking the bedroom door and taking the key with him. He stole some money from Miss Mulley's bag, and used it to buy a train ticket at Burton station.

At John Fenton's trial, it was revealed that the knife in Miss Mulley's neck had not hit any major blood vessels. The cause of her death was the wounds inflicted by the tin of sausages.

A lot of the trial was taken up by a discussion about the mental state of John Fenton. He had endured a sorry childhood. His father had committed suicide when the boy was 18 months old, and John had suffered from meningitis as a child, which may have affected his brain cells. The defence pointed out that when he broke into The Woodlands, he hadn't eaten for three days and his blood sugar would have been low. Medical evidence was produced that Fenton had abnormal reactions to low sugar levels. Dr Lescher of Derby Royal Infirmary said that he had come to the conclusion that the accused was 'of such low intelligence that he could be regarded as a child'.

A debate followed on the subject of whether John Fenton was capable of knowing what he was doing. The judge intervened to ask Dr Lescher, 'Do you believe that he knew what he was doing, when he struck Miss Mulley, qualified only by reason of the abnormally low intelligence, his childishness and the other factors you have enumerated which made him less capable of controlling himself?'The doctor replied that he did.

The jury retired and after 58 minutes, they brought in a verdict of guilty, but added a recommendation of mercy 'owing to mental immaturity'. The judge, Mr Justice Streatfeild, passed a death sentence, but four months later this was commuted to life imprisonment by the Home Secretary.

A POACHER HANGED TWICE

POACHING HAS ALWAYS SEEMED TO ME A STRANGE CRIME. A RABBIT RUNS ALONG A PUBLIC FOOTPATH, AND YOU CAN CATCH IT TO FEED YOUR FAMILY. IF IT VEERS A FEW FEET TO THE LEFT OR THE RIGHT, ONTO PRIVATE LAND, IT BECOMES THE PROPERTY OF THE LANDOWNER, AND IT BELONGS SOLELY TO HIM. IF YOU CATCH IT NOW, YOU ARE COMMITTING A CRIME. THE LANDOWNER WILL HIRE MEN TO PUNISH YOU FOR YOUR CRIME OF TRYING TO FEED YOUR CHILDREN.

Rural poverty and the need to put food on the family table led many men into poaching. The sworn enemies of the poacher were the gamekeepers. Thomas Smith junior often used to go out with a gamekeeper, James Bamford, on the hunt for poachers. Thomas was no ordinary gamekeeper's assistant. He was the son of the Lord of the Manor of Whiston Eaves, Thomas Smith senior, and therefore a man of some status in the area.

On Wednesday 4th July 1866, the two men were out all night, keeping a vigilant eye out for anyone out poaching in the area of Moneystone Common, near

Cotton. In order to cover a wider area, the two men split up and were patrolling about a mile apart. When Thomas failed to turn up at the prearranged meeting place the next morning, a search party was instigated. The searchers found clothing belonging to Thomas at Quarry Hole, and at 9.30am his dead body was found nearby, lying in a hollow in a wood. The son of the lord of the manor had been shot and battered about the head, causing a fracture of the skull. The blows looked as if they had been inflicted by a gunstock. Thomas Smith's hat, peppered with gunshot, lay nearby, still with a wild rose in the hatband.

The assumption was that he had been killed by a poacher, and the names of the local poachers were well known. They made their way to the home of William Collier. He had seven children, and the meat he obtained from his nocturnal poaching formed a large part of his family's diet. William was arrested and taken into custody. A shotgun found hidden in a drain near Collier's home was found to have dark hair adhering to the stock. A man from Hollington identified the gun as one he'd previously sold to William Collier.

At the trial, Thomas Webb, a surgeon from Cheadle, stated that he had examined William Collier's clothing and had found bloodstains on his collar and trousers. Collier was found guilty, but the jury recommended mercy. The judge was having no truck with this recommendation, however. The accused was an inveterate poacher, and the dead man was from the family of the local landowner. William Collier was sentenced to be hanged.

The hanging took place outside Stafford prison on 7th August. It was a remarkable occasion, because the hangman was not very proficient. When the trapdoor opened, William Collier dropped through it, followed by the entire rope. The hangman had not attached it to the crossbeam. There is a belief that if a hanging fails, then the condemned man is released as a free man. However, this belief is a myth. The groggy William Collier was brought out from beneath the staging, taken back up to the scaffold and hanged a second time. The crowd of spectators thought this unfair and booed the second hanging.

An interesting thing happened after I'd written about this story. A descendant of William Collier from Nottingham contacted me. He told me of a family tradition that one of William Collier's children was not his biological child, but was actually the son of Thomas Smith junior, the son of the local lord of the manor. Had Smith been exercising the droit de seigneur with the wife of William Collier? Perhaps the killing of Thomas Smith was not just a story of the poacher and the landowner, after all.

SAINTLY BILLY?

WILLIAM PALMER WAS BORN IN RUGELEY IN 1824. AFTER ATTENDING RUGELEY GRAMMAR SCHOOL, WHERE HE HAD THE REPUTATION OF BEING A SPENDTHRIFT WITH MONEY HE HAD BORROWED, HE WAS APPRENTICED TO A FIRM OF WHOLESALE CHEMISTS IN LIVERPOOL. WHILE HE WAS THERE HE SEDUCED THE DAUGHTER OF THE FAMILY WHERE HE LODGED, BUT IT WAS EMBEZZLEMENT RATHER THAN HIS OTHER ANTICS THAT LED TO HIS DISMISSAL. HE WAS CAUGHT OPENING THE FIRM'S LETTERS AND STEALING MONEY.

William returned to Staffordshire and began a career in medicine by being apprenticed to Dr Edward Tylecote in Great Haywood. He was still very fond of young ladies, and was ingenious in some of the ways he employed to be alone with the girls he fancied. He made a point of attending church regularly, but arranged to be frequently called out of the service to attend a sick patient. In reality, he was visiting his young mistress, Jane Widnall, while her parents remained safely ensconced in the church he had just left.

In 1846, William was sent to complete his training under a Dr Stegall in London. While in the metropolis, William lived a wild life of partying, gambling and womanising. Given William's extravagant and licentious lifestyle, it is somewhat surprising that he succeeded in completing his medical training and gained the Diploma of the College of Surgeons. It may be less surprising to learn that he failed to pay Dr Stegall the 50 guineas he had promised him for helping him pass his exams!

Dr Palmer returned to his native Rugeley and set up practice in a house in Market Street. He soon began to pay court to an eighteen-year-old girl named Ann Brookes who lived with her guardian in Abbots Bromley. Ann had been left a considerable sum of money by her late father, a colonel in the Indian Army, and this may well have been why William decided that on this occasion he would marry the girl. William and Ann were married at the church in Abbots Bromley in October 1847.

William Palmer had always been fond of horse-racing, and now he established a stable of racehorses, and arranged for them to be trained in Hednesford. His racing enterprises lost money continuously, and his debts grew larger.

A year after her marriage, Ann Palmer gave birth to a son. Four later children all died as babies, and their nurse stated publicly that she believed that Dr Palmer had killed them by putting sugar laced with poison on his finger for them to suck, because he couldn't afford to provide for them.

Other people connected with William Palmer also died unexpectedly. His mother-in-law died while visiting Palmer, immediately after lending him money. While at a race meeting, Dr Palmer gave medical attention to Mr Bly of Norfolk, to whom he owed £800. When Bly died, Palmer denied owing the money and told the dead man's wife that the debt was owed the other way, to himself.

It was at about this time that William Palmer insured his wife's life for £13,000. Ann Palmer died, and her death was recorded as being caused by cholera. Although William appeared to mourn his wife's death, it has to be noted that the housemaid, Eliza Tharme, bore him an illegitimate child just nine months after Ann's death. The baby was born in Dr Palmer's house but died six months later.

The insurance money from Ann's death was soon dissipated, and William tried to insure his brother Walter for £80,000. The insurance companies were suspicious of this large sum, and the eventual sum assured was smaller. Walter Palmer died very soon after the insurance was taken out. When Palmer tried to insure the life of a

The home of Dr Palmer in Rugeley. The young woman in the doorway is the housemaid, Eliza Tharme.

friend, George Bate, he could find no company willing to accept the proposal.

William was now desperate to obtain money. Apart from his many debts, he was being blackmailed by Jane Bergen, a young lady with whom he had had a torrid affair. Jane was threatening to show to her father – a Stafford policeman – Dr Palmer's very frank and salacious love letters.

One of Dr Palmer's racing cronies was John Parsons Cook of Lutterworth. Like Palmer, Cook was a professional man who preferred to spend his time and money at the racecourse. When one of Cook's horses won the Shrewsbury Handicap, it netted him £1,700.

After a celebration party in a Shrewsbury hotel, the two men returned to Rugeley. Cook took a room in the Talbot Arms Hotel, which was situated opposite Palmer's house.

Dr Palmer invited John to dinner, but after the meal the visitor was taken violently ill. The next day, William sent his sick friend some broth, but he was unable to eat it. A chambermaid thought it a pity to waste the broth and drank some, but it caused her to be sick. During the night Cook became desperately ill, shrieking and having convulsions until his body contorted into a rigid curve. He died in agony. William Palmer certified that his friend had died from apoplexy, and arranged for the body to be laid out immediately.

At the post-mortem, Cook's intestines and stomach were pronounced 'healthy', but Cook's stepfather was suspicious and insisted that the organs be sent to London for further analysis. The driver of the carriage engaged to transport the jar containing the organs was to claim later that Palmer offered him a bribe of £10 to upset the jar and spill its contents. Palmer seemed very anxious to know the result of the second analysis of Cook's stomach, and bribed the Rugeley postmaster Samuel Cheshire to open the letter from London containing the result. When he read that no poison had been found, William Palmer said, 'I knew it. I'm as innocent as a baby.'

The inquest heard that Dr Palmer had bought strychnine just before Cook's death and a verdict of wilful murder was brought in. William Palmer was arrested, and an order was made for the exhumation of his late wife and his brother. Their bodies were examined by Dr Alfred Taylor of Guy's Hospital; he concluded that Ann had probably died of antimony poisoning, though the evidence in the case of Walter Palmer was inconclusive.

However, it was solely for the murder of John Parsons Cook that Dr Palmer was tried. He should have been tried in Stafford, but because of the strong local feelings against Palmer, the Lord Chancellor brought in a bill to enable offenders to be tried away from the scene of their alleged crime, in certain circumstances. The Palmer Act is still in force today.

Dr William Palmer

The trial of Dr Palmer was therefore held at the Old Bailey in London, where the prosecution was led by the Attorney General. All of the evidence against Palmer was circumstantial, the prosecution case resting on the similarity between the symptoms shown by Cook as he died and those known to be caused by strychnine poisoning. After a twelve-day trial, William Palmer was found guilty of murder and sentenced by the judge, Lord Chief Justice Campbell, to be taken back to Stafford to be hanged in public.

At 8am on Saturday 14th June 1856, William Palmer was taken out to the scaffold, which had been erected outside Stafford prison, where crowds had been gathering since 3am. Many were there for the entertainment, the spectacle, and the thrill of being at such an important public event. In all, the crowd numbered over 30,000 people. The hangman was George Smith, a former inmate of Stafford prison who had volunteered to act as assistant hangman at the execution of James Owen and George Thomas 16 years earlier.

William Palmer shook hands with Smith, who then proceeded to place the rope around the doctor's neck. The bolt was drawn and Palmer dropped to his death. He was 31 years of age. His mother, who knew her son's vices only too well, never accepted his guilt on the murder charge. It was at this point that she came out with the wonderful comment, 'They have hanged my saintly Billy.' Many mothers regard their sons through rose-tinted spectacles and see them as lovely boys even though the rest of the world sees them as villains.

Some historians agree with her that Palmer's conviction may have been unsafe, alleging that the doctor's appalling record as a serial embezzler, womaniser and gambler made the public only too willing to believe him capable of killing, even though there was no real evidence that Cook had in fact been murdered. However, others believe that Palmer had committed far more murders than the one he was charged with.

There is one wry footnote to the case. After the Palmer case, so it is said, a number of eminent Rugeley men became disturbed that the name of their town would always be associated with 'Palmer the Poisoner'. They petitioned the prime minister of the day to ask whether Rugeley could be known by a different name. The prime minister replied that he was prepared to allow their request but only if the town could be named after him. The good townsfolk considered this alternative – Palmerston – and decided that they could live with the old name of Rugeley after all!

SUICIDE VIA THE HANGMAN

ON FRIDAY 25TH FEBRUARY 1955, DONALD LAINTON WAS DRIVING FROM STOCKPORT TO SUTTON COLDFIELD IN HEAVY SNOW. THE AA HAD TOLD HIM THAT THE MAIN ROADS WERE PASSABLE, BUT WHEN HE GOT INTO STAFFORDSHIRE, THE SNOW GOT WORSE AND HE GAVE UP HOPE OF CONTINUING HIS JOURNEY.

He pulled into the car park of the Coach and Horses Inn in the village of Great Haywood, and went in to see if he could get a meal. He found that they didn't do meals (this was 1955 after all), but the man who'd been playing the piano came over and said that he knew a pub where they did serve meals. After finishing their drinks, the two men got into Donald's car and drove off.

The car – a green Ford Prefect – was spotted at 1.45pm in a lane leading to Birchen Bower Farm, at Willslock, near Uttoxeter. It appeared to be stuck in a snowdrift, and a man was rocking the car backwards and forwards, as if to free it. A little later the car was still there, but the man had gone. At 3pm, the farmer's wife, Elizabeth Bettson, went down to have a closer look at the car. She saw blood on the door, and she caught a glimpse of a man's legs in the space behind the front seats. A milk tanker drove past, and Mrs Bettson asked the driver for help. The driver and his mate checked the car, and found a man covered with some overcoats. They drove off to the Red Cow pub to phone for help.

However, help arrived more quickly than they had hoped. Quite by chance, an ambulance manned by Ken Fallows and Alan Goodall drove past on its way from Burton to Uttoxeter. They stopped to help. The man in the car – Donald Lainton – was severely wounded, so they got him into the ambulance and, despite the snow-covered road, they decided to take him to Stafford Hospital. Ken later recalled: 'We used the ambulance like a snowplough. We must have pushed a ton of snow all the way to Stafford.'

At Stafford General Hospital the staff informed the police, who came to speak to him, but Donald Lainton died without regaining consciousness. A post-mortem revealed that he had died through shock and haemorrhage, following stab wounds to the head and chest. One wound had lacerated the lung; another had penetrated the eye and pierced the brain.

On the following Sunday, Fred Cross, a 33-year-old concrete moulder from Farley, was charged with the murder. He immediately admitted the crime, saying that he had stabbed Donald Lainton with half a pair of scissors, which he had thrown into a field after the killing. After murdering the 28-year-old insurance broker, he had walked to the village of Kingstone, and then hitched a lift in a lorry to Great Haywood, where he'd recovered his bike from the car park of the Coach and Horses before cycling home to Farley.

Asked if robbery was the motive, he totally denied it. He gave a bizarre explanation of his motive for the crime. He said that his wife had left him in early January for another man, taking their two children with her. He had begged her to return but she had refused. Alone in his Nissen hut home, he had brooded on his situation, then decided that he would kill himself. He even bought some rat poison for the purpose, but lacked the courage to take it. After meeting Donald Lainton on the Friday night in the Coach and Horses, he had conceived a desperate and chilling plan: to commit a murder and be hanged for it. He would commit suicide by getting the hangman to do the job for him! He said that he did not feel sorry for himself – he wanted to die – but he did express regret when he learned that his victim was a married man with a baby son.

Fred Cross's trial, held in Stafford on 5th July 1955, was remarkable in several respects. Firstly, he refused any legal representation in court and insisted on pleading guilty. The judge explained that this would mean that he would receive a death sentence, to which Cross replied, 'That is what I want.' Despite the fact that everything had to be repeated because Fred Cross was somewhat deaf, the whole trial lasted a mere eight minutes! Fred Cross got his wish, and was hanged in Winson Green prison on 25th July, exactly five months after his crime. He had achieved his aim of committing suicide via the hangman.

THE FATAL LOVE TRIANGLE

GWEN MASSEY LIVED ALL HER LIFE IN THE MOORLANDS VILLAGE OF RUDYARD, TWO MILES NORTH-WEST OF LEEK. SHE LIVED FIRST WITH HER PARENTS, THEN WITH HER GRANDPARENTS. SHE GAVE UP BEING A STUDENT NURSE AT NORTH STAFFORDSHIRE ROYAL INFIRMARY TO MOVE IN WITH AND CARE FOR HER ELDERLY GRANDPARENTS. HOWEVER, HER SOCIAL LIFE WAS NOT LIMITED TO VILLAGE ACTIVITIES, BECAUSE SHE HAD A FANTASTIC TALENT: A BEAUTIFUL OPERATIC SOPRANO SINGING VOICE.

This ability had been recognised at her Methodist chapel in Rudyard and her primary school in Leek. Later, she had received specialised singing training from Miss Lucy Hall of Stoke-on-Trent. At her very first music festival in Longton, Gwen Massey won her class. In the years that followed she competed in festivals all over the north, and at the prestigious Lytham St Annes festival, she won the soprano class and was then judged the most outstanding performer of the whole festival.

It was through her music that she met Frank Walton, a businessman who was 17 years her senior and a married

Gwen Massey
(H. Jones Alcock/Shirley Palin)

man. At one musical event in Biddulph, Gwen and Frank sang a duet together, and afterwards, Frank asked Gwen out for a drink. They became close friends, and then in 1958 they became lovers. Frank proved to be very possessive, however, and was jealous if Gwen spoke to other men. Gwen did not resent this: she interpreted Frank's jealousy as proof of the power of his love for her. Their affair lasted for four years until Frank's wife Mary discovered that he was being unfaithful. Mary did not ask about the identity of her husband's lover, but she did insist that he put an end to the affair.

Frank told Gwen they could no longer meet, but he did prolong their romance by ringing her up every day from work, thus keeping her affection alive. His insistence on keeping Gwen's feelings for him simmering below the surface led to a terrible consequence. On Friday 8th February 1963, after a telephone conversation, the two women – Gwen, who was 34, and Mary, 52 – agreed to meet at the Plough Inn in Endon at 7.30pm. After they had met and talked in Mary's car, they each drove their own car to Gwen's bungalow in Rudyard. Gwen put her car into the garage, and Mary Walton left her red Mini Traveller estate parked outside.

At some time during the evening, the women argued, and the argument turned into violence. Gwen Massey struck her rival a number of blows on the back of her head with a hammer, injuring her fatally. She then had to dispose of the unconscious, dying woman. She bundled her into the back of the Mini Traveller, then drove Mrs Walton's car for eleven miles along icy and snow-covered roads to the village of Mow Cop on the Cheshire border. She parked the car, and set off to walk back to her home. It was nearly midnight, and the weather was freezing. Gwen was wearing a fur coat, nylons and high-heeled shoes, completely unsuitable clothing for the moorlands in the middle of a freezing

February night. She must have walked for three or more hours, before finally reaching her Rudyard home.

The parked car was spotted in High Street, Mow Cop, by bus driver Reuben Austin the next day at 1pm. At 9.15pm it was still there, and he went to investigate. He saw the body in the back and rang for the police. It was not difficult to check the number plate and establish that it belonged to Mrs Mary Walton of Newcastle-under-Lyme, who had been reported missing on the Saturday afternoon.

The police removing bloodstained ice at Rudyard
(H. Jones Alcock/Shirley Palin)

Four witnesses came forward to report seeing the unusual sight of a lone woman walking between Mow Cop and Congleton between 11pm and midnight on the Friday night. A farmer's wife from Rudyard stated that she had seen a red estate car parked on the road by Gwen Massey's bungalow between 8pm and 10.15pm. The police found traces of blood on Gwen's path, and opposite her house they found bloodstained pieces of ice that had been shovelled up and thrown over a farm wall.

Gwen Massey was taken in for questioning. At first she denied killing Mrs Walton, but eventually she confessed to the crime, after being told that the death penalty would not apply in the case. At her trial in May, many questions were asked about the police interviews. Because Gwen had been interviewed as a witness, rather than as a suspect, she was never cautioned or advised that she need not make a statement. There was also a time when the male police superintendent sent the female police officer out to make a cup of tea, leaving him alone with Gwen. It was while they were alone that Gwen had made her final statement, admitting her guilt. Despite these deficiencies, the facts were not disputed, and the case went ahead.

Gwendoline Massey was found guilty of murder and given a life sentence. She proved a model prisoner and was released after serving six years.

THE DOG THAT DIDN'T BARK

WHEN FREDERICK WILTSHAW LEFT HIS POTTERY FACTORY – WILTSHAW & ROBINSON LTD – IN STOKE-ON-TRENT AT 4.15PM ON WEDNESDAY 16TH JUNE 1952, HE HAD NO IDEA OF THE HORROR THAT WAS WAITING FOR HIM AT HOME. AS USUAL HE CALLED IN AT TRENTHAM GOLF CLUB FOR A HAND OF BRIDGE BEFORE DRIVING BACK TO BARLASTON AT 6PM. WHEN HE ARRIVED AT HIS HOME, A FOURTEEN-ROOM DETACHED HOUSE NAMED ESTORIL, HE WENT INTO THE KITCHEN. A SAUCEPAN AND VEGETABLES HAD BEEN SPILLED AND THERE WAS BLOOD ON THE WALL AND FLOOR. IN THE HALL HE DISCOVERED THE BODY OF HIS WIFE, ALICE. HER FACE WAS BATTERED AND THERE WAS A BLOODSTAINED POKER NEXT TO HER.

He immediately rang a neighbour, Dr Harold Browne, who came round and confirmed that Alice was dead, before ringing the police. Frederick was asked to check if there had been anything stolen, but at that stage he thought that nothing was missing. Faced with the possibility that it was not a robbery, the police had to check out whether the death was due to domestic violence. They quickly established that Frederick had rung the doctor less than a minute after arriving home. The killing had almost certainly committed by an intruder.

Estoril House
(Derek Tatton)

Outside, they found that a wicket gate had been left open, and two heifers were trampling the garden at the rear of the house. A pair of bloodstained gloves was discovered under an apple tree.

Frederick Wiltshaw described the household routine at Estoril. Two maids came in from 8.15am until 3.30pm. Before they left, they always prepared vegetables and put them in a saucepan for Mrs Wiltshaw to cook for Frederick's dinner. A chauffeur-gardener, Roy Shenton, worked outside from 8am until 5.30pm. Two other men rented three acres of the grounds which they worked as a market garden. They were usually working until 5pm. All of these people were questioned.

The police established that Alice had been speaking to a friend on the phone until 5.22pm. The gardener had heard Mrs Wiltshaw calling the dog in at about five o'clock, and he was sure that the wicket gate was closed when he left at 5.25. Frederick had arrived home at 6.18pm to find his wife murdered. Alice must therefore have been killed at some time between 5.30 and 6.15. The police were puzzled that the Wiltshaw's dog, a toy poodle named Midge, renowned for her loud barking at strangers, had not been heard barking that evening. Was it possible that the killer was someone the dog already knew?

When the police established that Roy had only worked at Estoril for ten weeks, the previous chauffeur-gardener having been fired for unauthorised use of the car at weekends, they decided that they also needed to question his predecessor, Leslie Green. A detective sergeant was sent to his home in Longton to interview him. However, Green's wife told him that her husband no longer lived with her; he had run away with a nurse whom he had met in Leeds.

Leslie Green, the former gardener at Estoril (picture: Express & Star)

Meanwhile, Frederick had found that £3,000 worth of jewellery was missing from a box in the bedroom, and also two rings his wife always wore had been removed from her fingers by her killer. Leslie Green would have known the layout of the house. He would also have known the routine of the house: at what time the various members of staff left. He was also known to the poodle, who would not have barked at him. If Alice Wiltshaw had surprised him during a robbery, she would have recognised him. Was that why she had to be murdered?

At 9.15 the next morning, a cool and confident Leslie Green strolled into the police station at Longton and introduced himself as the man the police were looking for. He admitted that he had been sacked for using the Wiltshaws' car to visit his girlfriend in Leeds. He even owned up to booking a hotel room in Leeds using the name Leslie Wiltshaw of Barlaston. However, he had an alibi for the afternoon of the murder. He claimed that he had been in Stafford at the Station Hotel, drinking with the manager and three other men. At 5pm he had walked into the town centre, where he had 'slept it off' on a park bench for 45 minutes. He'd then returned to the hotel to wash and change. Afterwards he had caught the 7.07 train to Leeds.

The police checked the information he had given them and found that, although some of the times he'd provided were wrong, he still had an alibi. He had left the hotel at 4pm and returned to wash and change at 6.30pm. He had been away for an hour and a half. But since he had no car of his own, and since no cars had been stolen in Stafford that afternoon, how could he have travelled from Stafford to Barlaston, committed the murder, and travelled back?

Acting on a hunch, Detective Chief Superintendant Tom Lockley decided to test a theory. He went to Stafford railway station and caught the 5.10 train to Barlaston. Arriving at 5.40, he climbed over the fence and walked through fields to the wicket gate behind Estori.. That walk had taken him seven minutes, so the walk back would take another seven minutes, and he could catch the 6.05 train back to Stafford. That left a gap of eleven minutes at the Wiltshaws' house, enough time for Green to enter, steal the jewels, be caught in the act and kill Mrs Wiltshaw. Tom Lockley had broken Leslie's Green's alibi.

When the police traced Green's girlfriend, she was surprised to hear that the man she knew as Terry was in fact married and named Leslie. She told the police that she and Green were engaged and banns for their marriage had been published while they were in her home town of Belfast. She said that 'Terry' had shown her two diamond rings on the evening after the murder. These rings, which he had ripped from the dead fingers of Alice Wiltshaw a few hours earlier, were later found hidden in a flat where Green and his fiancée had stayed. At his trial, Leslie Green was found guilty of the murder of Alice Wiltshaw and sentenced to death. He was hanged at Winson Green prison in Birmingham on 23rd December 1952.

BIBLIOGRAPHY

Bell, David, *Staffordshire Murder Casebook*, Countryside Books 1996

Bell, David, *Staffordshire Tales of Mystery and Murder*, Countryside Books 2005

Corder, Nicholas, *Foul Deeds and Suspicious Deaths in Staffordshire and the Potteries*, Wharncliffe Books 2006

Gibson, Alan, *Staffordshire Legends*, Churnet Valley Books 2002